Handwriting Skills Simplified

Level C
Learning Cursive Writing

Featuring the new simplified Zaner-Bloser alphabet models

Editorial Production
Pagination/Ed Horcharik

Text Illustrations
Ed Francis

Cover Design
Elliot Kreloff, Inc.

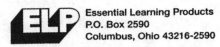 Essential Learning Products
P.O. Box 2590
Columbus, Ohio 43216-2590

TABLE OF CONTENTS

Page   **Content**

3   Basic cursive strokes/pencil position
4   Introduction to undercurve/ paper position
5   Undercurve letters i, u, w
6   Undercurve letters t, p, j
7   Undercurve letters r, s
8   Undercurve letters with loops e, l, b
9   Undercurve letters with loops h, k, f
10   Review: Undercurve letters
11   Evaluation: Slant
12   Introduction to overcurve
13   Introduction to overcurve
14   Overcurve letters n, m
15   Overcurve letters v, x
16   Overcurve letters y, z
17   Review: Overcurve letters
18   Evaluation: Size
19   Introduction to Downcurve
20   Introduction to Downcurve
21   Downcurve letters a, d, g
22   Downcurve letters q, o, c
23   Review: Downcurve letters
24   Evaluation: Shape
25   Review: Lowercase letters
26   Review: Lowercase letters
27   Uppercase/lowercase A
28   Uppercase/lowercase B
29   Uppercase/lowercase C
30   Uppercase/lowercase D
31   Review: A, B, C, D
32   Evaluation: Spacing
33   Uppercase/lowercase E

Page   **Content**

34   Uppercase/lowercase F
35   Uppercase/lowercase G
36   Uppercase/lowercase H
37   Review: E, F, G, H
38   Numerals 1-10
39   Uppercase/lowercase I
40   Uppercase/lowercase J
41   Uppercase/lowercase K
42   Uppercase/lowercase L
43   Review: I, J, K, L
44   Manuscript Maintenance
45   Uppercase/lowercase M
46   Uppercase/lowercase N
47   Uppercase/lowercase O
48   Uppercase/lowercase P
49   Review: M, N, O, P
50   Uppercase/lowercase letters Q
51   Uppercase/lowercase letters R
52   Uppercase/lowercase letters S
53   Uppercase/lowercase letters T
54   Review: Q, R, S, T
55   Review/Evaluation
56   Uppercase/lowercase letters U
57   Uppercase/lowercase letters V
58   Uppercase/lowercase letters W
59   Review: Checkstroke joinings
60   Uppercase/lowercase letters X
61   Uppercase/lowercase letters Y
62   Uppercase/lowercase letters Z
63   Review: U, V, W, X, Y, Z
64   Final Evaluation

BASIC CURSIVE STROKES

Short Undercurve
Touch the baseline; curve under and up to the midline.

Short Overcurve
Touch the baseline; curve up and right to the midline.

Tall Undercurve
Touch the baseline; curve under and up to the headline.

Tall Overcurve
Touch the baseline; curve up and right to the headline.

Short Downcurve
Touch the midline; curve left and down to the baseline.

Short Slant
Touch the midline; slant left to the baseline.

Tall Downcurve
Touch the headline; curve left and down to the baseline.

Tall Slant
Touch the headline; slant left to the baseline.

PENCIL POSITION

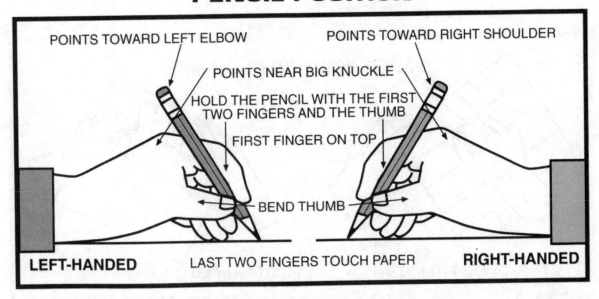

POINTS TOWARD LEFT ELBOW

POINTS TOWARD RIGHT SHOULDER

POINTS NEAR BIG KNUCKLE

HOLD THE PENCIL WITH THE FIRST TWO FINGERS AND THE THUMB

FIRST FINGER ON TOP

BEND THUMB

LEFT-HANDED

LAST TWO FINGERS TOUCH PAPER

RIGHT-HANDED

Introduction to
UNDERCURVE

Trace each backward oval without lifting your pencil or pen. Start at the dot.

Trace the undercurve-slant motion.

Write the undercurve-slant motion.

Write the joined undercurve-slant motion.

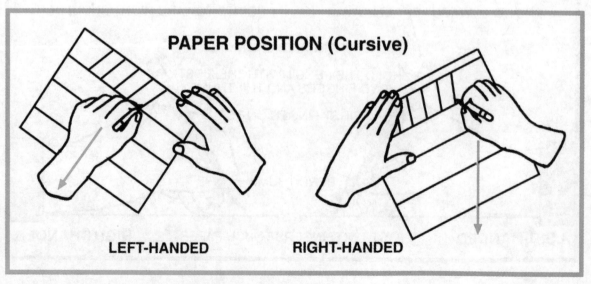

PAPER POSITION (Cursive)

LEFT-HANDED   **RIGHT-HANDED**

UNDERCURVE LETTERS

14 letters begin with the undercurve. Can you identify the letters that use the undercurve/slant motion?

Undercurve beginning letters

Trace and write these letters three times.

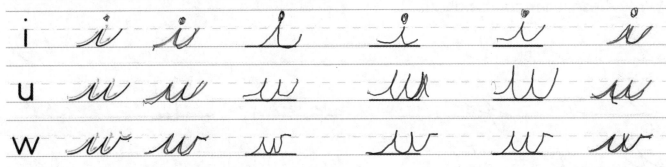

Write these letter combinations.

$u + i = ui$

The checkstroke is what we add to the u to make it a w. Trace and write the checkstroke-undercurve joining.

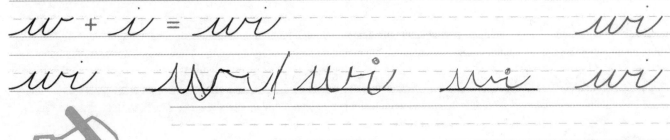

$w + i = wi$

PRACTICE

5

UNDERCURVE LETTERS

Trace and write these letters.

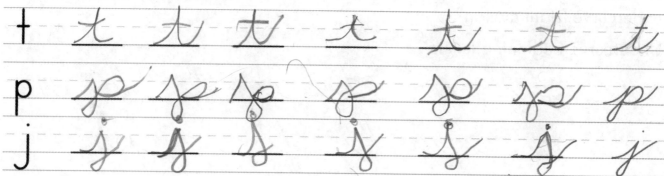

Write these letter combinations.

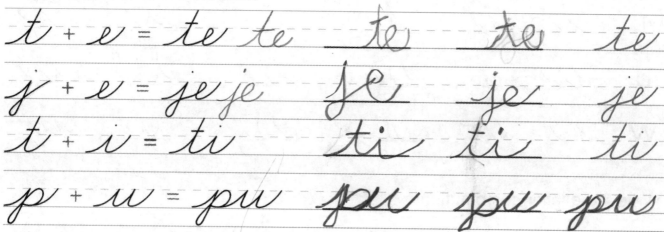

Write these words.

jet *jet* _____ _____

pure _____ _____

tile _____ _____

Trace and write these letters four times.

r _r_ _r_ _____ _____ _____ _r_

s _s_ _s_ _____ _____ _____ _s_

Write these letter combinations.

_s_ + _t_ = _st_ _____ _____ _st_

_r_ + _s_ = _rs_ _____ _____ _rs_

_t_ + _r_ = _tr_ _____ _____ _tr_

_e_ + _s_ = _es_ _____ _____ _es_

Write these words.

rest _____ _____

settler _____

street _____

RETRACE

A retrace happens when you backtrack over a line you already wrote. You must pause before you retrace.

CORRECT

INCORRECT

Write the lowercase **t**. Make a good retrace.

_t_ _____ _____ _____ _t_

7

UNDERCURVE LETTERS WITH LOOPS

Undercurve letters with loops.

e   l   b

Trace and write these letters.

e *e e _____ _____ _____ _____ e*

l *l l _____ _____ _____ _____ l*

b *b b _____ _____ _____ _____ b*

Write these letter combinations.

e + t = et _____ _____ et

b + e = be _____ _____ be

l + e = le _____ _____ le

Write these words.

enter _____ _____

later _____ _____

because _____

8

UNDERCURVE LETTERS WITH LOOPS

Trace and write these letters.

h   *h*   *h*   ___ ___ ___ ___   *h*

k   *k*   *k*   ___ ___ ___ ___   *k*

f   *f*   *f*   ___ ___ ___ ___   *f*

Write these letter combinations.

f + i = fi   ___ ___ ___   *fi*

h + i = hi   ___ ___ ___   *hi*

k + i = ki   ___ ___ ___   *ki*

Write these words.

file   ___ ___ ___

hike   ___ ___ ___

kite   ___ ___ ___

PRACTICE

UNDERCURVE LETTERS

Write each word. Make good joinings. Check height of letters.

sit _____ _____ _____

ties _____ _____ _____

feel _____ _____ _____

kite _____ _____ _____

wire _____ _____ _____

bell _____ _____ _____

tree _____ _____ _____

hers _____ _____ _____

better _____ _____ _____

fire _____ _____ _____

silk _____ _____ _____

hill _____ _____ _____

add _____ _____ _____

put _____ _____ _____

jest _____ _____ _____

SLANT

Check slant by drawing lines through letters.

CORRECT *good slant*

INCORRECT *little hill*

Write each letter two times. Draw lines through the letters to check for slant.

u _____ _____ *w* _____ _____

t _____ _____ *p* _____ _____

h _____ _____ *f* _____ _____

Write each word. Check for slant.

letter _____ _____

shelf _____ _____

feel _____ _____

pile _____ _____

shift _____ _____

EVALUATION

SLANT

STUDENT EVALUATION		TEACHER EVALUATION	
Correct	Incorrect	Correct	Incorrect
☐	☐	☐	☐

INTRODUCTION TO OVERCURVE

Trace each forward oval without lifting your pen or pencil. Start at the dot.

Trace the overcurve.

Write the overcurve.

Trace and write the slant-overcurve motion.

PRACTICE

INTRODUCTION TO OVERCURVE

The overcurve is part of the forward oval motion. Here are the six letters that begin with the overcurve. Notice how the overcurve is combined with the slant stroke.

Overcurve beginning letters

n m v x y z

Trace the overcurve-slant motion.

Write the overcurve-slant motion four times.

Write three overcurve-slant motions without lifting your pencil.

Write the overcurve-slant-undercurve motion.

OVERCURVE LETTERS

Write these letters.

n n n _____ _____ _____ n

m m m _____ _____ _____ m

Write these letter combinations.

$n + e = ne$ _____ _____ ne

$m + b = mb$ _____ _____ mb

$m + n = mn$ _____ _____ mn

$e + m = em$ _____ _____ em

$n + s = ns$ _____ _____ ns

Write these words.

$mist$ _____ _____

$limb$ _____ _____

$pens$ _____ _____

$fine$ _____ _____

$nest$ _____ _____

OVERCURVE LETTERS

Trace and write these letters. Note the checkstroke on the **v**.

v *v v* ___ ___ ___ *v*

x *x x* ___ ___ ___ *x*

Write these letter combinations.

v + e = ve ___ ___ *ve*

i + x = ix ___ ___ *ix*

x + e = xe ___ ___ *xe*

v + a = va ___ ___ *va*

Write these words. Make sure you make good checkstroke joinings.

exit ___ ___

river ___ ___

vase ___ ___

veil ___ ___

fix ___ ___

ax ___ ___

OVERCURVE LETTERS WITH DESCENDERS

Trace and write these letters. Notice how the descending part of the letter fills the entire space below the baseline.

y *y y* _____ _____ _____ _____ *y*

z *z z* _____ _____ _____ _____ *z*

Write these letter combinations.

y + *e* = *ye* _____ _____ *ye*

z + *y* = *zy* _____ _____ *zy*

b + *y* = *by* _____ _____ *by*

z + *e* = *ze* _____ _____ *ze*

Write these words.

size _____ _____

yellow _____ _____

bye _____ _____

buzz _____ _____

lady _____ _____

fuzzy _____

yak _____ _____

16

OVERCURVE LETTERS

Write each word.

minute _____

live _____ _____

mix _____ _____

yell _____ _____

buzz _____ _____

tiny _____ _____

bump _____ _____

trim _____ _____

nine _____ _____

maximum _____

minimum _____

liver _____ _____

Write this sentence.

I fix many vans.

I

SIZE

Writing has good size when all the letters touch the baseline and all letters of the same size are even in height.

Tall Letters

b d f h k l t

Short Letters

a c e g i j m n o

p q r s u v w x y z

CORRECT

balloon

INCORRECT

follow

Write these words with the correct size cursive.

play

mister

camp

tennis

likes

EVALUATION

SIZE

STUDENT EVALUATION
Correct   Incorrect

☐   ☐

TEACHER EVALUATION
Correct   Incorrect

☐   ☐

INTRODUCTION TO DOWNCURVE

The downcurve is part of the backward oval motion introduced on p.4. Here are the downcurve letters. Find the downcurve in each of these letters.

Downcurve beginning letters

a d g q o c

Trace the backward oval motion without lifting your pencil or pen.

Trace the downcurve.

Write the downcurve.

Write the downcurve-undercurve-slant stroke motion.

INTRODUCTION TO DOWNCURVE

Write backward ovals on the black lines without lifting your pencil and draw slant lines in each.

Trace the downcurve-undercurve to overcurve motion.

Write these motions on the black lines.

Join backwards ovals.

a d g

DOWNCURVE LETTERS

Trace and write these letters. Notice how the overcurve of the "g" crosses the slant stroke at the baseline.

a a a _____ _____ a

d d d _____ _____ d

g g g _____ _____ g

Write these letter combinations two times.

d + a = da _____ _____ da

a + g = ag _____ _____ ag

g + i = gi _____ _____ gi

g + a = ga _____ _____ ga

a + d = ad _____ _____ ad

Write these words.

hedge _____

again _____

digit _____

add _____

gate _____

DOWNCURVE LETTERS

Trace and write these letters.

q *q* *q* ___ ___ ___ ___ *q*

o *o* *o* ___ ___ ___ ___ *o*

c *c* *c* ___ ___ ___ ___ *c*

Write these letter combinations.

q + u = qu ___ ___ *qu*

c + o = co ___ ___ *co*

o + c = oc ___ ___ *oc*

c + a = ca ___ ___ *ca*

o + r = or ___ *or*

o + b = ob *ob*

Write these words.

quiet ___ ___

cozy ___ ___

form ___ ___

job ___ ___

cage ___ ___

DOWNCURVE LETTERS

Write each word.

add _____ _____ _____

grow _____ _____ _____

catch _____ _____ _____

quart _____ _____ _____

rodeo _____ _____ _____

order _____ _____ _____

cattle _____ _____ _____

quit _____ _____ _____

Write these joinings two times.

ba _____ _____ *ba*

wo _____ _____ *wo*

oa _____ _____ *oa*

op _____ _____ *op*

ad _____ _____ *ad*

23

SHAPE

Keep the loops open in the letters **b**, **f**, **h**, **k**, **l**, and **e**.

CORRECT

b   f   h   k   l   e

INCORRECT

b   f   h   k   l   e

Close the ovals in the letters **a**, **d**, **g**, **q**, and **o**.

CORRECT

a   d   g   q   o

INCORRECT

a   d   g   q   o

Write this sentence. Be sure to keep loops open and ovals closed. Evaluate for shape.

I have good loops and ovals.

EVALUATION

SHAPE

STUDENT EVALUATION		TEACHER EVALUATION	
Correct	Incorrect	Correct	Incorrect
☐	☐	☐	☐

LOWERCASE LETTERS A–N

Write these manuscript and cursive letters.

a __ _a_ __   b __ _b_ __

c __ _c_ __   d __ _d_ __

e __ _e_ __   f __ _f_ __

g __ _g_ __   h __ _h_ __

i __ _i_ __   j __ _j_ __

k __ _k_ __   l __ _l_ __

m __ _m_ __   n __ _n_ __

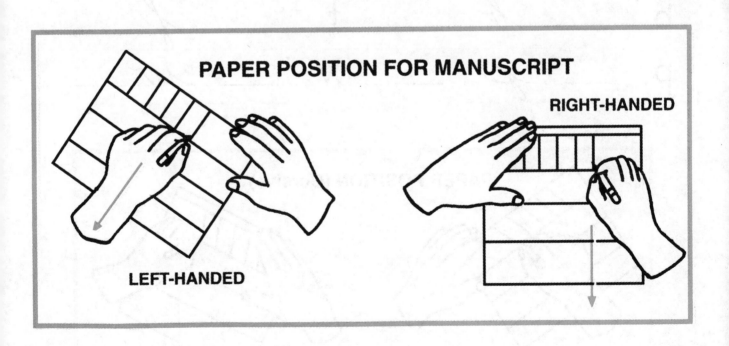

PAPER POSITION FOR MANUSCRIPT

RIGHT-HANDED

LEFT-HANDED

LOWERCASE LETTERS O–Z

Write these manuscript and cursive letters.

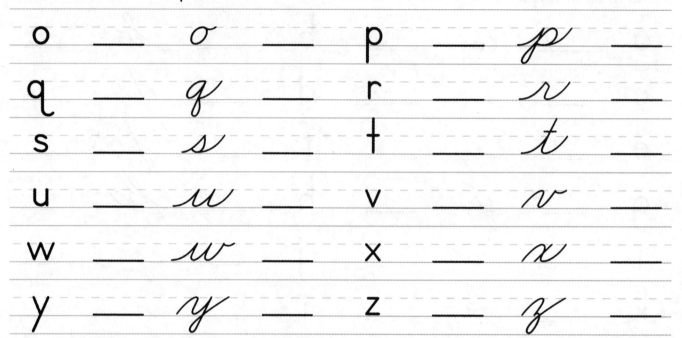

o	—	_o_	—	p	—	_p_	—
q	—	_q_	—	r	—	_r_	—
s	—	_s_	—	t	—	_t_	—
u	—	_u_	—	v	—	_v_	—
w	—	_w_	—	x	—	_x_	—
y	—	_y_	—	z	—	_z_	—

Practice these letters.

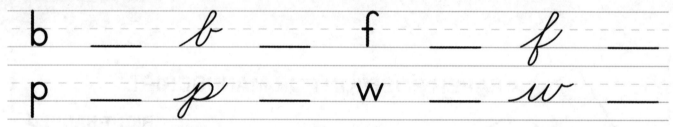

| b | — | _b_ | — | f | — | _f_ | — |
| p | — | _p_ | — | w | — | _w_ | — |

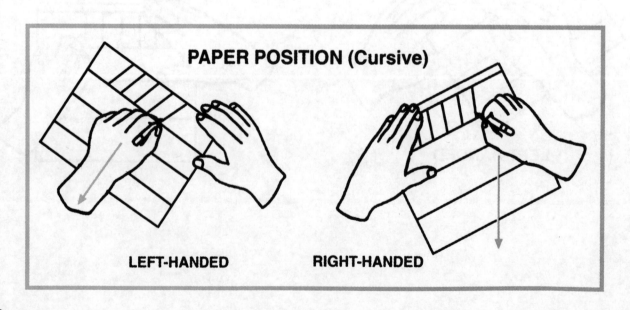

PAPER POSITION (Cursive)

LEFT-HANDED   **RIGHT-HANDED**

Upper- and Lowercase
LETTERS

Write the lowercase **a**.

a _ _ _ _ _ *a*

Write each word.

parade _____

pajamas _____

banana _____

Trace and write the uppercase **A**.

A *a a* _ _ _ _ *a*

a _ _ _ _ _ *a*

Write each word.

Asia _____ _____

Ann _____ _____

American _____

Alabama _____

Alaska _____

Arizona _____

Upper- and Lowercase
LETTERS

Write the lowercase **b**.

b _____ _____ _____ _____ _____ *b*

Write each word.

bubble _____

babies _____

birth _____

scrub _____

Trace and write the uppercase **B**.

B *B* *B* _____ _____ *B*

B _____ _____ *B*

Write each word.

Beth _____ _____

Bill _____ _____

Bombay _____

Boston _____ _____

28

Upper- and Lowercase
LETTERS

c C

Write the lowercase **c**.

c _ _ _ _ _ _ _ _ *c*

Write each word.

crack _____ _____

catch _____ _____

check _____ _____

cocoa _____ _____

Trace and write the uppercase **C**.

C C C C _ _ _ _ _ *C*

C _ _ _ _ _ _ *C*

Write each word.

China _____ _____

Carl _____ _____

Clara _____ _____

Chicago _____

Upper- and Lowercase
LETTERS

Write the lowercase **d**.

d _ _ _ _ d

Write each word.

riddle

ladder

decide

daddy

Trace and write the uppercase **D**.

D D D _ _ _ _ D

D _ _ _ D

Write each word.

Dan

Dot

David

Denver

A THROUGH D

Write each letter two times.

a _____ _____   *B* _____ _____

C _____ _____   *D* _____ _____

a _____ _____   *b* _____ _____

c _____ _____   *d* _____ _____

Write these letter combinations.

Ca _____ _____ _____ _____ *Ca*

Ab _____ _____ _____ _____ *Ab*

Ad _____ _____ _____ _____ *Ad*

ac _____ _____ _____ _____ *ac*

Ch _____ _____ _____ _____ *Ch*

ba _____ _____ _____ _____ *ba*

Cr _____ _____ _____ _____ *Cr*

bu _____ _____ _____ _____ *bu*

31

SPACING

Rules for correct spacing:
1. Letters should be evenly spaced.

CORRECT

spacing

INCORRECT

crowded   *open*   *varying*

2. Words should be evenly spaced. This is how you check your spacing. Undercurve and overcurve beginning words

going home is not

Downcurve beginning words.

six cats ate all

3. The space between sentences should be even. This is how you check your spacing.

went. I will go.

Write these sentences in cursive. Evaluate for spacing.

The French are famous for their food.

EVALUATION

SPACING

	Correctly Spaced	Crowded	Open
Are your words	☐	☐	☐
Are your letters	☐	☐	☐

32

Upper- and Lowercase
LETTERS

Write the lowercase **e**.

e _ _ _ _ _ _ *e*

Write each word.

every _____ _____

screen _____ _____

entire _____ _____

erect _____ _____

Trace and write the uppercase **E**.

E *E* *E* _ _ _ _ *E*

E _ _ _ _ _ _ *E*

Write each word.

Erma _____ _____

Ed _ _ _ _ _

England _____

Erie _____ _____

Write the lowercase **f**.

f ___ ___ ___ ___ ___ *f*

Write each word.

fan _____ _____

fifth _____ _____

fluff _____ _____

raffle _____ _____

Trace and write the uppercase **F**.

F *F F* ___ ___ ___ ___ *F*

F ___ ___ ___ ___ *F*

Write each word.

Frank _____ _____

France _____ _____

Florida _____

Friday _____

Upper- and Lowercase
LETTERS

Write the lowercase **g**.

_g_ ___ ___ ___ ___ ___ _g_

Write each word.

giggle _____ _____

guest _____ _____

gang _____ _____

general _____

Trace and write the uppercase **G**.

G _G_ _G_ ___ ___ ___ ___ _G_

_G_ ___ ___ ___ ___ ___ _G_

Write each word.

Gail _____ _____

Gus _____ _____

Greg _____ _____

Georgia _____

Upper- and Lowercase
LETTERS

Write the lowercase **h**.

h _____ _____ _____ _____ *h*

Write each word.

hush _____ _____

where _____ _____

they _____ _____

hatch _____ _____

Trace and write the uppercase **H**.

H *H* *H* _____ _____ _____ *H*

H _____ _____ _____ _____ *H*

Write each word.

Helen _____ _____

Hank _____ _____

Haiti _____ _____

Havana _____

E THROUGH H

Write each letter two times.

$\mathcal{E}$ ___ ___ e ___ ___

$\mathcal{F}$ ___ ___ f ___ ___

$\mathcal{G}$ ___ ___ g ___ ___

$\mathcal{H}$ ___ ___ h ___ ___

Write these letter combinations.

$\mathcal{E}a$ ___ ___ ff ___ ___

$\mathcal{H}a$ ___ ___ he ___ ___

$\mathcal{H}e$ ___ ___ fl ___ ___

$\mathcal{E}r$ ___ ___ ng ___ ___

$\mathcal{E}d$ ___ ___ ft ___ ___

Write the question mark.

? ? ___ ___ ___ ___ ___ ___ ?

NUMERALS

Trace and write these numerals.

1   1   1   ⎯   ⎯   ⎯   ⎯   1

2   2   2   ⎯   ⎯   ⎯   ⎯   2

3   3   3   ⎯   ⎯   ⎯   ⎯   3

4   4   4   ⎯   ⎯   ⎯   ⎯   4

5   5   5   ⎯   ⎯   ⎯   ⎯   5

6   6   6   ⎯   ⎯   ⎯   ⎯   6

7   7   7   ⎯   ⎯   ⎯   ⎯   7

8   8   8   ⎯   ⎯   ⎯   ⎯   8

9   9   9   ⎯   ⎯   ⎯   ⎯   9

10   10   10   ⎯   ⎯   ⎯   ⎯   10

Practice writing these numbers.

$12 + 34 = 46$

$13 + 10 = 23$

$14 + 1 = 15$

$9 - 2 = 7$

$2 \times 4 = 8$

Upper- and Lowercase LETTERS

Write the lowercase **i**.

i _____ _____ _____ _____ _____ *i*

Write each word.

icicle _____ _____

oil _____ _____

lick _____ _____

inning _____ _____

Trace and write the uppercase **I**.

I *I* *I* ____ ____ ____ *I*

I _____ _____ _____ *I*

Write each word.

India _____ _____

Ivan _____ _____

Idaho _____ _____

Irene _____ _____

39

j *J*

Write the lowercase **j**.

j   —   —   —   —   —   *j*

Write each word.

job

jewel

jeans

enjoy

Trace and write the uppercase **J**.

J *J* *J* — — — —   *J*

J — — — — —   *J*

Write each word.

Jack

Judy

Japan

Jersey

Upper- and Lowercase
LETTERS

Write the lowercase **k**.

k _____ _____ _____ _____ *k*

Write each word.

skate _____ _____

bake _____ _____

kayak _____ _____

khaki _____ _____

Trace and write the uppercase **K**.

K *K K* _____ _____ _____ *K*

K _____ _____ _____ _____ *K*

Write each word.

Keith _____ _____

Kathy _____ _____

Kansas _____

Kentucky _____

41

l L

Upper- and Lowercase
LETTERS

Write the lowercase **l**.

l _____ _____ _____ _____ _____ l

Write each word.

lovely _____ _____

calm _____ _____

full _____ _____

lullaby _____ _____

Trace and write the uppercase **L**.

L L L _____ _____ _____ L

L _____ _____ _____ _____ L

Write each word.

Linda _____ _____

London _____ _____

Lassie _____ _____

Louis _____ _____

I THROUGH L

Write each letter two times.

I _____ _____ *i* _____ _____

J _____ _____ *j* _____ _____

K _____ _____ *k* _____ _____

L _____ _____ *l* _____ _____

Write these letter combinations.

Ki _____ _____ *al* _____ _____

Ji _____ _____ *kh* _____ _____

Jo _____ _____ *ly* _____ _____

Je _____ _____ *ck* _____ _____

sk _____ _____ *oi* _____ _____

ng _____ _____ *il* _____ _____

Write the exclamation point.

! *!* _____ _____ _____ _____ _____ *!*

Write these sentences. Evaluate for the four "Ss": Size Shape Spacing Slant.

Throw it to me.

Can you catch it?

I think I can.

Then get ready.

Perfect catch!

EVALUATION

THE FOUR Ss

SPACING		SLANT	
Correct	Incorrect	Correct	Incorrect
☐	☐	☐	☐

SHAPE		SIZE	
Correct	Incorrect	Correct	Incorrect
☐	☐	☐	☐

Upper- and Lowercase LETTERS

Write the lowercase **m**.

m _ _ _ _ _ _ _ _ *m*

Write each word.

mark _____ _____

mint _____ _____

memory _____

mom _____ _____

Trace and write the uppercase **M**.

M m m _ _ _ _ _ _ *m*

m _ _ _ _ _ _ _ _ *m*

Write each word.

Maria _____ _____

Mike _____ _____

Maine _____ _____

n *n*

Write the lowercase **n**.

n ___ ___ ___ ___ *n*

Write each word.

inner _____ _____

bone _____ _____

none _____ _____

nation _____

Trace and write the uppercase **N**.

N *n* *n* ___ ___ ___ *n*

n ___ ___ ___ ___ *n*

Write each word.

Neil _____ _____

Norma _____ _____

Nevada _____

Newport _____

Upper- and Lowercase
LETTERS

o O

Write the lowercase **o**.

o ___ ___ ___ ___ ___ *o*

Write each word.

spool ___ ___

boot ___ ___

alone ___ ___

odor ___ ___

Trace and write the uppercase **O**.

O O O ___ ___ ___ *O*

O ___ ___ ___ ___ *O*

Write each word.

Ohio ___ ___

Ollie ___ ___

Omaha ___ ___

Oslo ___ ___

Write the lowercase **p**.

p _ _ _ _ p

Write each word.

poppy

happen

paper

pepper

Trace and write the uppercase **P**.

P P P _ _ _ P

P _ _ _ P

Write each word.

Pedro

Paula

Paris

Poland

48

M THROUGH P

Write each letter two times.

m ___ ___ m ___ ___

n ___ ___ n ___ ___

o ___ ___ o ___ ___

p ___ ___ p ___ ___

Write these letter combinations.

mo ___ ___ opo ___ ___

ni ___ ___ oc ___ ___

Me ___ ___ nn ___ ___

pp ___ ___ pa ___ ___

do ___ ___ lo ___ ___

Write the comma.

___ ___ ___ ___ ___ ___ ___ ___ ___ ___

Upper- and Lowercase
LETTERS

Write the lowercase **q**.

q _ _ _ _ _ _ _ *q*

Write each word.

quiet _____

equal _____

lacquer _____

quality _____

Trace and write the uppercase **Q**.

Q Q Q _ _ _ *Q*

Q _ _ _ *Q*

Write each word.

Quebec _____

Queen _____

Quito _____

Quaker _____

Upper- and Lowercase
LETTERS

Write the lowercase **r**.

r ___ ___ ___ ___ *r*

Write each word.

furry _____ _____

horn _____ _____

rare _____ _____

reader _____ _____

Trace and write the uppercase **R**.

R *R* *R* ___ ___ ___ *R*

R ___ ___ ___ *R*

Write each word.

Roberto _____ _____

Roman _____ _____

Raleigh _____

s S

Upper- and Lowercase
LETTERS

Write the lowercase **s**.

s ___ ___ ___ ___ ___ ___ s

Write each word.

less _____ _____

smile _____ _____

seals _____ _____

sash _____ _____

Trace and write the uppercase **S**.

S S S ___ ___ ___ S

S ___ ___ ___ ___ S

Write each word.

Sally _____ _____

Susan _____ _____

Steven _____ _____

Spain _____ _____

52

Upper- and Lowercase
LETTERS

Write the lowercase **t**.

t _ _ _ _ _ _ *t*

Write each word.

title _____ _____

tablet _____ _____

total _____ _____

tooth _____ _____

Trace and write the uppercase **T**.

T T T _ _ _ _ *T*

T _ _ _ *T*

Write each word.

Tim _____ _____

Tina _____ _____

Turkey _____

Teresa _____ _____

Write each letter two times.

Q _____ _____ q _____ _____

R _____ _____ r _____ _____

S _____ _____ s _____ _____

T _____ _____ t _____ _____

Write these letter combinations.

Ra _____ _____ re _____ _____

Re _____ _____ ti _____ _____

qu _____ _____ to _____ _____

ot _____ _____ cq _____ _____

st _____ _____ sm _____ _____

Ro _____ _____ rr _____ _____

ta _____ _____ rs _____ _____

Write these sentences. Evaluate for the four "Ss": Size Shape Spacing Slant.

The Queen of England reads all the reports that are sent to her. Her trips are reported in the press.

EVALUATION

STUDENT EVALUATION			TEACHER EVALUATION	
Correct	Incorrect		Correct	Incorrect
☐	☐	**SLANT**	☐	☐
☐	☐	**SHAPE**	☐	☐
☐	☐	**SIZE**	☐	☐
☐	☐	**SPACING**	☐	☐

u U

Upper- and Lowercase LETTERS

Write the lowercase **u**.

u _____ _____ _____ _____ *u*

Write each word.

tune _____ _____

build _____ _____

umpire _____ _____

unruly _____ _____

Trace and write the uppercase **U**.

U *U U* _____ _____ _____ *U*

U _____ _____ _____ *U*

Write each word.

Utah _____ _____

Uncle _____ _____

Uranus _____

Uganda _____

Upper- and Lowercase
LETTERS

Write the lowercase **v**.

v — — — — — *v*

Write each word.

vase ————— ————

wavy ————— ————

valve ————— ————

video ————— ————

Trace and write the uppercase **V**.

V *V V* — — *V*

V — — *V*

Write each word.

Violet ————— ————

Vernon ————— ————

Virginia —————

Upper- and Lowercase
LETTERS

Write the lowercase **w**.

w _____ _____ _____ _____ *w*

Write each word.

wigwam _____

town _____

waffle _____

grow _____

Trace and write the uppercase **W**.

W *W* *W* _____ _____ *W*

W _____ _____ _____ *W*

Write each word.

Will _____

Wendy _____

Washington _____

Wyoming _____

58

LOWERCASE JOININGS

Checkstroke joining are difficult because they change the shape of the letter that follows the checkstroke. With practice, however, you can make rapid and legible checkstroke joinings.

Lowercase letters that require checkstroke joinings.

b   o   v   w

Checkstroke to short undercurve   *b e be bean*

Checkstroke to tall undercurve   *w l wl awl*

Write each word four times.

bind

vulture

lawful

window

operate

blonde

vendor

blown

wring

ounce

x X

Write the lowercase **x**.

x _ _ _ _ _ _ *x*

Write each word.

exit _____ _____

oxen _____ _____

wax _____ _____

vixen _____ _____

Trace and write the uppercase **X**.

X X X _ _ _ _ X

X _ _ _ _ X

Write each word.

X-out _____ _____

X-ray _____ _____

Xmas _____ _____

Chicken Pox _____

Upper- and Lowercase
LETTERS

Write the lowercase **y**.

y —— —— —— —— —— *y*

Write each word.

yard —————— —————— ——

young —————— —————— ——

asylum —————— ——————

destroy —————— ——————

Trace and write the uppercase **Y**.

Y Y Y —— —— —— —— *Y*

Y —— —— —— —— —— ——

Write each word.

Yukon —————— ——————

New York ——————————

Yolanda ——————————

South Yemen ——————————

Write the lowercase **z**.

z _ _ _ _ *z*

Write each word.

zebra

dizzy

zigzag

dazzle

Trace and write the uppercase **Z**.

Z *Z Z* _ _ _ *Z*

Z _ _ _ *Z*

Write each word.

Zeke

Zulu

Zack

U THROUGH Z

Write each letter two times.

$\mathcal{U}$ _____ _____ u _____ _____

$\mathcal{V}$ _____ _____ v _____ _____

$\mathcal{W}$ _____ _____ w _____ _____

$\mathcal{X}$ _____ _____ x _____ _____

$\mathcal{Y}$ _____ _____ y _____ _____

$\mathcal{Z}$ _____ _____ z _____ _____

Write these letter combinations.

$\mathcal{U}n$ _____ _____ $\mathcal{U}g$ _____ _____

$\mathcal{Y}e$ _____ _____ zz _____ _____

$\mathcal{Z}o$ _____ _____ ax _____ _____

$\mathcal{Z}y$ _____ _____ wn _____ _____

gz _____ _____ vy _____ _____

sy _____ _____

Before doing the following assignment, review these page for the standards of legible handwriting (4 "Ss"): Slant, p.12; Size, p.18; Shape, p.24; Spacing, p.32.

1. In cursive handwriting, tell why it is important to have legible handwriting.

2. At the bottom of your essay, print in manuscript today's date and your teacher's name.

3. Then write your signature in your best cursive handwriting.

4. Finally, evaluate your handwriting in the evaluation box below. And then ask your teacher to evaluate your writing.

EVALUATION

STUDENT EVALUATION			TEACHER EVALUATION	
Correct	Incorrect		Correct	Incorrect
☐	☐	**SLANT**	☐	☐
☐	☐	**SHAPE**	☐	☐
☐	☐	**SIZE**	☐	☐
☐	☐	**SPACING**	☐	☐